P9-CCB-296

The Living Desert

By Dinah Brown

MODERN CURRICULUM PRESS

Pearson Learning Group

Credits

Photos: All photos © Pearson Learning unless otherwise noted.

Front cover: E.R. Degginger/Color-Pic, Inc. Title page: Terry Donnelly/Dembinsky Photo Associates. 5: Wolfgang Kaehler. 9: Fred Hirschmann. 10, 11: E.R. Degginger/Color-Pic, Inc. 12: Bjorn Backe/Papilio/Corbis. 13: T.A. Wiewandt/DRK Photo. 14: Stan Osolinski/Dembinsky Photo Associates. 15: Fred Hirschmann. 17: W. Wayne Lockwood M.D./Corbis. 18: John Gerlach/DRK Photo. 19: Art Wolfe. 20: E.R. Degginger/Color-Pic, Inc. 21: George H.H. Huey. 22: Clive Druett/Papilio/Corbis. 23: Michael & Patricia Fogden/Corbis. 24: Stephen J. Krasemann/DRK Photo. 25: E.R. Degginger/Color-Pic, Inc. 26: Stan Osolinski/Dembinsky Photo Associates. 27: Galen Rowell/Corbis. 28: Michael & Patricia Fogden/Corbis. 29, 30: E.R. Degginger/Color-Pic, Inc. 31: Susan E. Degginger/Color-Pic, Inc. 32, 33: E.R. Degginger/Color-Pic, Inc. 34: Bettmann/Corbis. 35: Stan Osolinski/Dembinsky Photo Associates. 36: E.R. Degginger/Color-Pic, Inc. 37: Jeff Foott/DRK Photo. 39: John Cancalosi/DRK Photo. 40: W. Perry Conway/Corbis. 41: Sharon Cummings/Dembinsky Photo Associates. 43: Phil Degginger/Color-Pic, Inc. 44: T.A. Wiewandt/DRK Photo. 45: E.R. Degginger/Color-Pic, Inc. 46: Fred Hirschmann.

Illustrations: 6–7: Mapping Specialists.

Cover and book design by Lisa Ann Arcuri

ISBN 0-7652-2169-1
Printed in the United States of America
8 9 10   11 10 09 08

Modern Curriculum Press
Pearson Learning Group

1-800-321-3106
www.pearsonlearning.com

Contents

For Eliza and Isabella

Chapter 1

A Hot Home

A desert is one of the hottest, driest places on Earth. Daytime air temperatures can stay over 100 degrees Fahrenheit for months at a time. Ground temperatures are even higher. That's hot!

There is almost no rain to bring any relief from the heat. A desert usually gets no more than 10 inches of rain throughout a whole year. That's barely enough to wet the ground.

Deserts are dry, hot, and sandy.

Fierce winds often blow across deserts. They make the heat and lack of water feel even worse. The winds may be light whirlwinds that spin across the desert. They can also be strong windstorms. The strong winds feel like air blown from a giant hair dryer set at its hottest setting. They dry up the moisture in plants and in the skin of animals.

Strong winds pick up sand when they blow over a desert's sandy areas. Then the wind-blown sand forms a thick cloud. The wind can blow this sand hard enough to strip paint off cars.

The winds can be so strong that they actually shape the desert. The blown sand forms hills, or dunes. These dunes grow and shrink as the wind blows. The sand seems to move along in ripples that look like waves across the desert floor. Sand-filled wind carves rock into unusual shapes.

There are deserts in Africa, China, Australia, the Middle East, and North and South America. Some deserts are rocky, while others are made up mostly of sand. Some have mountains, and others are mostly flat.

The United States has several deserts. They are all found in the western part of the country. The largest desert areas are found in Nevada, Utah, California, Wyoming, and Arizona.

One of the most interesting deserts in the United States is the Sonoran Desert. This desert is one of the hottest areas in North America. Its summer daytime temperatures normally exceed 100 degrees. Winter temperatures average about 60 degrees. The area is fairly flat with low hills.

CANADA

N
W — E
S

ATLANTIC OCEAN

exas

0   250   500 miles
0   250   500 kilometers

Desert

Desert areas in the United States

It's hard to imagine how anything could live in such a hot and dry place. However, lots of plants and animals live in the Sonoran Desert. They have adapted, or adjusted, in many different ways to survive the heat, the wind, and lack of water.

All living things need water to live. All animals have water in their bodies. There's water in skin, blood, and all the tissue that make up a body's muscles, heart, lungs, and other organs.

There is water in plants, too. Roots suck up water from the ground. Then the water moves through a plant's stem, branches, and leaves.

Desert plants get and store water in different ways. Many of them have long roots. The roots spread out to find water underground. In some plants the stems expand like balloons to store any water they get.

Plants also lose a lot of water by evaporation through their leaves. This means that warm, dry air around the leaves causes the water inside them to turn into a gas and evaporate into the air. Many desert plants don't have leaves so they won't lose water in that way. Instead, they have thin, sharp needles. Needles hold moisture better than leaves. They also help protect a plant from animals that might try to take water stored in the plant's stem.

Many plants grow and bloom in the desert, especially in the spring.

The animals find water in different ways, too. Some get it by eating plants. Others have bodies that need very little water. Many of the animals hide from the heat so they won't lose water from their bodies through evaporation. They dig dens or burrows beneath the ground. Temperatures there are cooler. Many of these animals don't come out to search for food until nighttime. The air is much cooler then. Some spend the day resting in the shade of large plants.

When it does rain, the desert changes. Flowers bloom. Animals that are usually scarce are very active during the few days following a rain.

At first sight the Sonoran Desert may look like a dry and lonely place. If you take a closer look, you'll see that it is filled with life. Wait until just after the sun sets. Look under bushes. Watch to see what comes up from burrows underground. You may just decide that the desert is a wonderful place to call home.

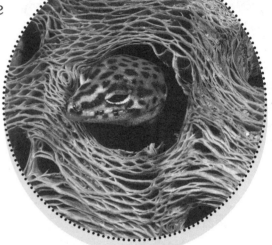

A banded gecko hides from the sun's heat in the remains of a chollo cactus.

Hot Fact   **The highest temperature ever recorded on Earth was 136 degrees Fahrenheit. This was in the desert in Libya, a country in northern Africa. The highest temperature recorded in the United States was 134 degrees in Death Valley, California.**

Chapter 2
Desert Cacti and Bushes

Looking around the Sonoran Desert, you won't see evergreens or trees covered with bright green leaves. Instead, you will see cacti and scraggly-looking bushes and trees. These and other plants in the desert can survive with very little water.

Cacti grow in the Sonoran Desert.

Saguaro cactus

The biggest plants you'll find in the desert are cacti. Some are tall and spiky. Others are big and round. All cacti hold onto every drop of water they get.

The Saguaro cactus is the biggest and tallest living thing in the Sonoran Desert. This kind of cactus can grow as tall as 50 feet. It may have 50 "arms" or branches growing from its main stem. It takes several years for the cactus to grow its first arm. The largest Saguaro cacti can be 200 years old. How do they grow so big with so little water?

A Saguaro cactus spreads its roots over an area as wide as it is tall. These roots take up any moisture in the ground and send it up into the plant. The outer layer of the cactus expands like an accordion to store the water. When the cactus is full, it can store up to a ton of water. As the water is used, the cactus shrinks.

A Saguaro cactus also grows very slowly. It may grow no more than one inch per year. In this way, it uses its stored water very slowly.

Plants also need water to bloom. With all the water held inside a Saguaro cactus, it blooms every year, even without rain. For about one month a year, the tips of the stems bloom with flowers of creamy-white petals. Each flower blooms just once. It opens in the evening after the sun has set and closes around noon the next day.

The Saguaro grows juicy fruit from its flowers. The three-inch, oval fruit is green on the outside. Inside there's bright-red pulp, juice, and as many as 4,000 seeds. Desert creatures and people find this fruit a wonderful treat to eat.

Saguaro
cactus flowers

Barrel cactus

The barrel cactus is another large cactus in the Sonoran Desert. It's not as tall as the Saguaro cactus, but it is very wide. It looks like a gigantic barrel.

Like the Saguaro, the barrel cactus has ribs, or pleats, all around it. Water soaked up by the roots fills the ribs. To hold more water, the ribs expand, making the cactus look like a bulging barrel. These ribs also channel the rain to fall directly under the plant where its roots can soak up every drop.

The barrel cactus protects the water it stores. Thick clusters of spines grow along the ribs. The spines keep away any animals that might try to dig into the cactus to get at the water that's inside it. One type of barrel cactus, the fishhook barrel cactus, has spines that are bent at the ends like fishhooks. Any animal that gets one of these stuck in its skin or fur will have a hard time getting it out.

The pulp inside a barrel cactus is sweet and can be made into candy. Because of this some people have named the cactus a candy barrel cactus. The fruits of this cactus are juicy, but not as good to eat as the pulp. Native Americans have long used both the pulp and the fruits. After digging the pulp out of the cactus they also made cooking pots out of the barrel.

Like the Saguaro cactus, the barrel cactus grows very slowly. It sometimes grows as little as one quarter of an inch per year. It's not surprising that most barrel cacti don't grow any taller than ten feet.

Barrel cactus fruit

Some plants survive in the Sonoran Desert because of their smell. The smell of the creosote bush is sweet to some people. Others like to call it the "little stinker." Happily for the creosote bush, many insects and animals in the desert don't like its smell, either. They leave it alone instead of trying to eat it.

You'll rarely see other plants growing around the creosote bush. The bush produces a deadly substance that spreads through the soil around it. That way the creosote bush does not have to compete with other plants for the little water that's in the soil.

The creosote bush also has a complex root system to help it survive in the dry desert. It brings in water through two sets of roots. One set is shallow and spreads out right under the ground. The other set of roots grows much deeper.

The creosote bush closes its pores in the daytime so that it won't lose water. Pores are very small holes in the leaves. The bush, like all plants, takes in carbon dioxide and gives off oxygen through the pores. At night the pores of the creosote bush open so that it can absorb, or bring in, any moisture that might be in the air.

Creosote bush

The branches of the creosote bush are gray with black rings all along each branch. Whenever an old piece of stem dies, a new one grows around the old. Creosote bushes can live for a long time by growing this way. Some creosote bushes have lived for nearly 100 years.

The cacti and bushes of the desert provide the shade and moisture that allow lots of animals to live comfortably in the desert. A snake may hide under a creosote bush when the sun is hottest. Jackrabbits sit in the shade of a Saguaro cactus to stay cool. Birds such as the Gila woodpecker and the northern flicker dig out small holes in the stems and trunks of plants. There they make a cool, moist home.

A northern flicker looks out from its home in a Saguaro cactus.

Hot Fact Just like some cacti, roses have thorns on their stems to help keep animals from eating them. Roses and cacti are in the same plant family.

Chapter 3

Desert Nightlife

The best time to see the many animals that live in the desert is at night. Most desert animals are nocturnal. That is, they sleep during the day and are active at night. By waiting until after the sun sets, the animals are active when the desert is coolest. Let's meet some of these nighttime prowlers.

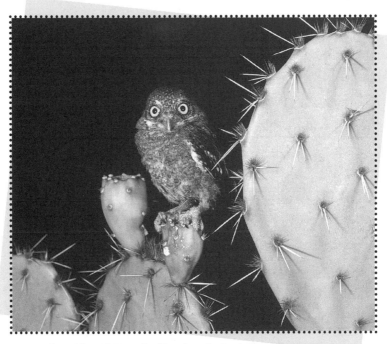

An elf owl is only five to six inches tall. It hunts at night for insects.

Banded gecko

"Gecko, gecko, gecko." That's a sound you would hear in the Sonoran Desert at night. It's the cry of a gecko calling. This little lizard is named for its high-pitched call. The gecko is quiet during the day. It stays cool by hiding in the shade or in a moist crack in a rock.

Most geckos are small, often just four to eight inches long. Their heads are big in relation to their bodies. The toes at the end of each of their four legs have suction pads. These allow them to stick to and climb rocks. Some people call them wall climbers.

If a gecko is frightened, it will stand as tall as it can on its legs. Then it waves its big tail back and forth to try to scare off whatever is threatening it.

The gecko's tail is not only good for scaring off enemies. It also stores up lots of fat that the gecko can use for energy in the winter months. Then there aren't as many insects, spiders, or baby scorpions around for the gecko to eat. The gecko slows down during the cold months, too. It can live for several months on the fat it stores in its long tail.

Western banded gecko

There are monsters in the Sonoran Desert, too. The Gila monster is large for a lizard. It can grow over 12 inches long. It has colorful black and orange, pink, red, or yellow beaded scales.

The Gila monster is one of only two poisonous lizards in the world. Usually it creeps through the dusty desert slowly on its four small legs. When it wants to bite something, it moves very quickly. The Gila monster attacks snakes, rats, insects, and other lizards for food. It will attack a human only if it feels threatened.

Like the gecko, the Gila monster captures most of its food in the summer months. It stores food in the form of fat in its large tail. Then it lives off the fat during the winter when food is scarce.

Gila monster

Sidewinder
rattlesnake

If you hear a rattle in the desert, watch out! It will likely be another desert animal– a poisonous rattlesnake. On the ends of their tails, rattlesnakes have small, hard segments. These bump against each other and make a rattling sound when the snake moves. The sound warns people and animals not to come any closer or they may be bitten. A rattlesnake usually adds one segment every year. So a snake with several rattles is old.

Sidewinders are a kind of desert rattlesnake. They got their name from their strange way of moving around the sandy desert. They go sideways instead of straight ahead. They raise a loop of their body, wind it around, drop the loop to the ground, and roll themselves forward. They're quick enough to catch mice, lizards, and even birds.

Like other desert snakes, sidewinders do not need to search for water. They get all the water they need from the animals they eat. So sidewinders live comfortably in the desert.

The desert jackrabbit is another Sonoran Desert animal. It spends its days in the shade of a bush or giant cactus and doesn't come out until nightfall. The desert jackrabbit is the only jackrabbit that is nocturnal. Like other rabbits, the desert jackrabbit eats grasses, plants, and other vegetation.

Most rabbits have big, floppy ears. The ears of the desert jackrabbit are especially big. These big ears help the jackrabbit stay cool. When the jackrabbit is sitting in the shade, its warm blood is cooled by the surrounding air as it circulates through the jackrabbit's big ears.

Jackrabbits are among the fastest runners and jumpers in the desert. When they are frightened, they can usually outrun a bobcat or coyote. This is a good defense since those animals would find the jackrabbit a tasty dinner.

Desert jackrabbit

These animals, and many others, are most active during the desert's cool nighttime temperatures. Some spend the hottest part of the day under bushes and cacti. Others find a much cooler spot by going underground. After roaming the desert all night, many desert animals escape to cool burrows or dens during the day.

Diamondback rattlesnake

Hot Fact Rattlesnakes are found only in North and South America. They live in most of the United States. However, the largest number are found in the Southwest.

Underground in the Desert

Many Sonoran Desert animals have a good reason for living under the ground. The ground just under the hot surface is much cooler and wetter. The desert is covered with the holes of dens and burrows dug by animals. Some of these holes are very big and some are quite small. Some may be hard to see because the animal inside has closed the entrance with rocks and dirt to keep in the cool, moist air.

A ground squirrel comes out of its burrow.

Desert tortoise

Desert tortoises dig many homes in the ground. Different tortoises may use these homes at different times. Some of the homes may be several feet wide. Such a large home gives the average 15-inch tortoise plenty of room. Here the tortoise stays for much of its life. It comes out only for water or to nibble on plants.

When the desert tortoise needs a drink of water, it digs more holes to collect rainwater. The tortoise seems to sense when rain is coming. You might see a tortoise waiting by one of its holes as the clouds build and get ready to rain. After it drinks the water in one hole, the tortoise will move on to another hole. The tortoise remembers where all of its holes are. After drinking its fill, the tortoise's body can hold a lot of water to be used during drier times.

Kangaroo rat

Having a cool, moist home is also important to the kangaroo rat. It escapes the hot, drying sun by spending its days surrounded by the cool, moist soil in its burrow. It comes out only at night. Even then the kangaroo rat seems to be most active only between 9 P.M. and 3 A.M. At that time there is the most moisture in the air.

The kangaroo rat never takes a drink of water. It makes its own water. The rat's body is able to use the water in the seeds it eats.

The kangaroo rat got its name from its long back legs. The rat uses its legs to jump far in any direction to get away from an enemy such as a rattlesnake. If it can't jump far enough, it may use its back legs to kick sand in the enemy's face.

Coyotes are one of the largest Sonoran Desert animals. They dig their dens in the ground or find a space under a rocky ledge. These spots are a coyote's cool home away from the hot sun.

Coyotes are smart, fierce hunters. They are members of the dog family, with keen hearing and great speed. A hungry coyote can sometimes catch even a fast-running jackrabbit.

Some people call the coyote's cry the sound of the desert. Its sharp barks echo through the desert at night. They can sometimes be heard during the day, too.

Coyotes call to each other when they hunt in packs. They also bark to warn other animals to stay out of their territory.

Some animals of the desert don't have to dig to make the underground homes they live in. For example, the sidewinder moves into the burrow that belonged to the animal it just ate. Coyotes, bobcats, cougars, and bats will move into small caves. Some animals take over a burrow another animal has left. Then they fight to keep the original owner out.

A cougar looks out from a small cave.

Hot Fact An underground den holds more moisture when an animal is living in it. Invisible, tiny droplets of water in the animal's breath are trapped inside the den in the form of moist air.

Chapter 5

Basking in the Sun

Not all animals of the Sonoran Desert try to stay out of the sun. Some animals spend the day out in the sun's heat. On a summer day in the desert, you may see lizards and iguanas stretched out on rocks, basking in the sun. On rocky ledges, you might see bighorn sheep standing against the desert sky. Wild burros may cross the desert without having to stop for water.

Wild burros

Desert iguana

Many reptiles run about the desert during the day. Reptiles are a group of animals whose blood is not naturally warm like a mammal's blood. Some reptiles are snakes, lizards, iguanas, and turtles. They all depend on the sun for body heat.

The desert iguana is one animal that can stay out in daytime heat up to 115 degrees. It stays active searching for food and looks out for enemies waiting to make a meal of it. Most lizards will attack and eat other animals. An iguana eats only plants and grasses.

On the rare days that are hotter than 115 degrees, the desert iguana will move into the cooler shade of a creosote bush. The desert iguana is hard to see under the bush. Its spotted brown, gray and reddish skin pattern blends in with the colors of the bush and the desert soil.

Black-collared
lizard

A black-collared lizard is another reptile that will warm itself on a rock in the sun. When the rock gets too hot, it will skitter away to find another rock that is in the shade.

The black-collared lizard is sometimes called a tiny dinosaur. When threatened, it will stand on its two hind feet to run. Sometimes it runs to catch insects. Other times it runs to get away from something that has disturbed it.

Its name comes from the black or black-and-white striped collar that can be seen across the back of the lizard's neck. The rest of the lizard is a spotted tan or olive color. These colors blend in with the desert ground.

Burros used to carry packs for prospectors
who were looking for gold.

Bigger animals can also survive in the Sonoran Desert's heat during the day. The burro is one of these animals. As it travels, the burro eats plants and grasses. It can get some water from the plants it eats. It does not need much, but when it is thirsty, it searches for the small pools that sometimes form near rocks.

The burros were brought to the Sonoran Desert by people. Long ago, people crossed the desert in search of gold. Burros carried their packs. These hardy animals often outlived the people who owned them. Sometimes the burros escaped and wandered farther into the desert. From these burros, wild burros were born. Today, many wild burros roam the desert. Others are still used by people to carry things.

The desert bighorn sheep is another large daytime hunter. The males are called rams and the females are called ewes. The rams have large brown horns that curl around their ears.

For most of the year, the bighorn sheep spend their days on rocky cliffs. They nibble at grasses and search for water to drink. At night they curl up and sleep. Only during very hot days do they rest during the day and come out at night. These sheep stay away from people, so it is rare to see them.

The bighorn sheep is named for its large horns.

Coatis are little animals that look like raccoons. They travel around the Sonoran Desert in groups. They chatter to each other as they search for food. They hunt in the daytime all through the year and don't seem to mind the heat of the summer. A coati eats all the time. It gets the water it needs from the lizards, insects, and cactus fruit it eats.

Coati

Hot Fact **Many animals that spend the day out in the desert sun have pale skin, fur, or feathers. Lighter colors take in less heat from the sun than darker colors. So having a pale color helps to keep an animal from getting too hot.**

Chapter 6
On the Move

Throughout the Sonoran Desert, creatures skitter and scurry and hop and race as they search for food and escape their enemies. Many of these animals move very quickly. Bobcats race across the dusty, sandy ground. Roadrunners whiz by. Even smaller animals, like the tarantula, are known for their speed.

A roadrunner runs more than it flies.

The roadrunner is a bird that runs and runs. It can race across the desert at 18 miles an hour. This bird is usually about two feet tall. It is a funny-looking member of the cuckoo family. The roadrunner wiggles oddly as it runs. It can hold its big body in the air just long enough to fly for a short time. That's only when it's going downhill.

Once in a while the roadrunner rests. In the middle of a summer day, this quick bird will stop, bob its tail up and down, and wait for the temperature to cool as the sun sets. Then it's off again in search of the small animals, such as insects, birds, and lizards, that it eats.

The roadrunner is quick enough to surprise and catch even a rattlesnake as it basks in the sun. There aren't many animals in the desert that can do that. The roadrunner has an unusual way of hunting a rattlesnake. It will hop all around the snake so that the snake will strike. The snake has a hard time hitting the roadrunner's skinny legs, especially when they are moving so fast. Finally, the snake tires. Then the roadrunner uses its long, sharp beak to stab the snake in the head.

The roadrunner often swallows its prey in one gulp. A rattlesnake, though, is a big mouthful. The roadrunner swallows as much as it can. Then it lets the rest of the snake hang out of its beak. The roadrunner continues its day digesting the bit of rattlesnake in its stomach. When there's more room in its stomach, the roadrunner swallows more of the snake.

A roadrunner catches a lizard.

You would probably hear a bobcat before you actually saw it. Some people say its deep growl is the most frightening sound in the Sonoran Desert. From a distance the bobcat looks like an oversized housecat with a very short tail.

The bobcat is a fierce hunter. Even though it weighs only 15 to 20 pounds, it is able to kill animals as large as a deer. In the desert it lives on jackrabbits, ground squirrels, rats, mice, and sometimes deer. The bobcat usually hunts at night, but animals aren't safe from the bobcat during the day either.

Desert bobcat

Desert tarantula

Tarantulas are large spiders. They are faster than they look. That's how they survive in the Sonoran Desert. Unlike most spiders, the tarantula does not weave a web to catch its food. The tarantula jumps after its food, moving very quickly.

The desert tarantula does not jump far when it hunts, maybe just a few inches. However, it jumps so fast that its prey often doesn't see the spider coming. The desert tarantula eats insects, beetles, grasshoppers, other small spiders, and sometimes a scorpion.

The desert tarantula is only two or three inches long. Its eight long legs and body are covered with hair, making it look fearsome. However, tarantulas are not as dangerous as they look, at least not to people. It's true that they are poisonous. A tarantula injects poison into its prey to kill it. If a tarantula bites a human, there isn't enough poison to do more than cause swelling and itching.

Hot Fact The roadrunner is so common and so popular in New Mexico that it is the state bird.

Chapter 7

After the Rain

Rare rainfalls bring sudden change to the Sonoran Desert. The desert often gets a good rainfall in early spring. Then wildflowers suddenly appear across the desert ground.

Rain fills ponds that are dry the rest of the year. Almost as soon as it appears, a pond is filled with animal life. As soon as the pond dries up, the animals are nowhere to be found. How does this happen?

Plants bloom near a desert pond filled by rain.

There are lots of toads that live on riverbanks and in ponds outside the desert. There are also toads that live in the desert. Desert toads sleep through the dry months. They sleep deep in the ground where there's more moisture.

When rain creates ponds, the desert toad comes out of the ground. The desert toad breeds and lays its eggs before the pond dries up. This is also the only time the desert toad can eat food and drink water. Then it has to eat and drink enough to last through the dry months that follow.

A desert toad comes out of the mud after it rains.

Brine shrimp

Shrimp are another surprising animal to find in the desert. The fairy shrimp or the brine shrimp live very short lives. Their eggs survive through the dry months. Then, as soon as the rain falls and a pond forms, the eggs hatch. The new shrimp live their entire lives during the short life of the pond. During this time the shrimp lay more eggs that must wait to come to life until the next rain falls.

Wildflowers bloom in brilliant colors after a desert rainfall. Many flowers pop up in ditches or along roadsides where water collects. Many flowers also spring up in cracks between rocks on hillsides where there is soil and moisture.

A desert sunflower is one of these colorful wildflowers. It has a bright yellow flower on top of a one- to three-foot stem. Desert lilies grow from a bulb that can wait several years for enough rainfall to grow. The desert five-spot has pinkish petals that grow to form globelike flowers. They seem to glow when the sun shines through the flowers.

The flowers are not only beautiful. They are an important food source for the insects and small animals of the Sonoran Desert. Bees and birds collect the flowers' pollen, and birds and small animals eat the seeds.

Desert lily

The Sonoran Desert may seem harsh, but it is filled with creatures that have learned how to live on its stark dry land. They have discovered ways to keep cool when the blazing sun is high in the sky. They have all learned ways to find water and food. The desert is definitely a place full of life.

Hot Fact **The desert soil is far from lifeless. A handful of soil can contain dozens of flower seeds. They wait for rain so they can grow. In the Sonoran Desert a small area of desert soil contains on average 5,000 to 10,000 seeds.**

Glossary

adapted	[uh DAP tud] changed to fit new conditions
breeds	[breedz] gives birth to young; reproduces
circulates	[SUR kyuh layts] moves along a certain path and returns to the same point
complex	[kahm PLEKS] not simple; made up of many parts
creosote	[KREE uh soht] an oily liquid with a sharp smell from the plant of the same name
digesting	[dye JEST ihng] changing food in the stomach so that its nutrients can be used by the body
evaporation	[ee vap ur AY shun] the process by which water becomes a vapor or a gas
oval	[OH vul] shaped like an egg, an elongated circle
poisonous	[POY zun us] capable of harming or killing if taken into the body
scales	[skaylz] thin, flat, or beaded hard plates that cover and protect fish and reptiles